Activity Book 1 **Puzzle**

**Written by
Dave Kirkby**

This Puzzle Maths
Activity Book 1
is based on the
Puzzle Maths
Series 1 unit
of television
programmes in the
TVM series which
was produced for
Channel 4 Schools
by Double Exposure.

Introduction

Puzzles and games are fascinating and highly motivating and are enjoyed by everyone. The games and activity pages in this book are designed to capitalise on this. They are intended to be used with 7–9 year olds and to support the **Puzzle Maths** Series 1 in the Channel 4 Schools mathematics series **TVM**.

The general aim of this book is to provide a stimulating mix of games and activities to develop number work in the classroom and to support the National Numeracy Strategy. Key areas within the 'number' and 'shape and space' areas of the primary mathematics curriculum are targeted. Children need help in developing confidence and ability in mental mathematics and in using pencil and paper methods without the support of calculators. The activities in this book also aim to support this kind of work.

The book is divided into five sections, each of which supports and extends the content of the television programmes:

▶ Place Value and Ordering

▶ Adding and Subtracting

▶ Multiplication and Division

▶ Reasoning About Numbers

▶ Shape and Space

The book can also stand alone to support work in these areas independently of the programmes. Each section includes five games and activity sheets which allow for differentiated use and which can be easily adapted for use with children working individually, in pairs, in groups or as a whole class. As far as possible the activities use equipment which is normally available in schools. Some activities make use of the resource sheets which are at the back of the book. Each section begins with a teacher page which gives an overview of the activities that follow as well as some extension material for each activity.

© 1998
Channel Four Learning Ltd

All rights reserved

The activity pages within this publication may be photocopied for use within the purchasing institution only.

Written by Dave Kirkby
Edited by Liz Meenan and Alec Edgington
Designed by Andrew Barron & Collis Clements Associates
Illustrated by Cedric Knight

Further information about Channel 4 Schools programmes and accompanying resources is available from

Channel 4 Schools
PO Box 100
Warwick
CV34 6TZ

Contents

Place Value and Ordering

	Teacher's notes	3
1.1	Ghost trains	4
1.2	Ordering game	5
1.3	Match the digits	6
1.4	Make your choice	7
1.5	Words and 4-digit numbers	8

Adding and Subtracting

	Teacher's notes	9
2.1	Making 14	10
2.2	Satellite take-away game	11
2.3	Animal words	12
2.4	Target challenge	13
2.5	Magic squares	14

Multiplying and Dividing

	Teacher's notes	15
3.1	Fishing game	16
3.2	Multiplication patterns	17
3.3	Doubling machine	18
3.4	Grid multiplying	19
3.5	Target 24	20

Reasoning About Numbers

	Teacher's notes	21
4.1	Missing digits	22
4.2	Filling spaces	23
4.3	Number machines	24
4.4	Questions and answers	25
4.5	Three ways	26

Shape and Space

	Teacher's notes	27
5.1	Make a dice	28
5.2	Looking for triangles	29
5.3	Tangram puzzle	30
5.4	Name that shape	31
5.5	Perimeters	32

Resource Sheets

1	1–100 square	33
2	Number cards	34
3	Dotty grids	35
4	Multiplication patterns	36

Place Value and Ordering

Teacher's notes

1.1 Ghost trains page 4

Aims

To give practice in:
- ordering a set of 2-digit numbers
- recognising the value of each digit in a 2-digit number

Children can write each set of numbers on cards or pieces of paper, then order them in a line, before recording the numbers on the sheet. If they have difficulty in ordering the numbers, let them try locating their position on a 1–100 number line marked in tens.

Extensions

- Write down the difference between each adjacent pair of ordered numbers.
- Round each number to the nearest 10.
- Order sets of 3-digit numbers. Make 20 cards, each containing a different 3-digit number. Shuffle them and deal out four sets of 5 cards. Arrange each set in order. Collect them together and repeat the activity.

1.2 Ordering game page 5

Aims

To give practice in:
- ordering three 2-digit numbers
- recognising and using '<' notation
- developing strategies based on reasoning about numbers

An ordinary dice generates only the numbers 1 to 6. In order to generate all digits you could use a dice numbered from 0 to 9, or a set of number cards (0 to 9) shuffled and placed face down in a pile.

Discuss with the children the fact that the tens digit dominates the units digit; so if the tens are in order then the 2-digit numbers will be in order. After each round of the game, encourage the children to find the best arrangement of the six digits, particularly for the Game 2 variation. Use number cards to help in this.

Extensions

- If the three numbers are in order, score the difference between the first and last numbers.
- Change the game to involve ordering two 3-digit numbers.

1.3 Match the digits page 6

Aims

To give practice in:
- reading and writing 3-digit numbers

Before playing the game, children can practice reading the numbers, and matching them using number cards.

The more difficult numbers are those which contain a zero digit, like 805 and 460.

Extensions

- Let the children create their own 'Match the digits' scoresheet, writing down eight different numbers. They must include some which have a zero digit.
- Write the eight numbers in order from smallest to largest.
- Match each number with base-10 material.

1.4 Make your choice page 7

Aims

To give practice in:
- recognising the value of each digit in a 3-digit number
- ordering 3-digit numbers
- rounding 3-digit numbers to the nearest 100

Emphasise that in each round the children can choose three cards and discard one. The discarded card does not have to be the same each time.

Children may need help answering questions 9 to 11. Use a 100-division number line marked in tens, and in question 9, for example, label the ends of the line 400 and 500. Locate the numbers between 400 and 500 on the line and see how far away from 500 they are. Repeat with numbers between 500 and 600.

Extensions

- Repeat the activity with a different choice of four digits.
- Make the nearest 3-digit number to 100, to 200, to 300, ... to 1000.
- Investigate how many different 3-digit numbers can be made from the four cards. (There are 24.) Put them in order.

1.5 Words and 4-digit numbers page 8

Aims

To give practice in:
- reading and writing 4-digit numbers
- recognising the value of each digit in a 4-digit number

Before the activity, give children practice in reading and writing 4-digit numbers in words.

Numbers without a zero digit are usually easiest for children to write in words. Generally the more zeros there are the fewer words are used. For example: 3027 (5 words), 5400 (4 words), 5000 (2 words).

Extensions

- Try the same activity with 3-digit numbers. What different numbers of words are possible? Extend to 5-digit numbers.
- Investigate how many letters there are in the number words.

Place Value and Ordering

1.1 Ghost trains

▶ Write each set of numbers in order from smallest to largest.

Place Value and Ordering

1.2 Ordering game

Round					Score
1	☐☐	< ☐☐	< ☐☐		..............points
2	☐☐	< ☐☐	< ☐☐		..............points
3	☐☐	< ☐☐	< ☐☐		..............points
4	☐☐	< ☐☐	< ☐☐		..............points
5	☐☐	< ☐☐	< ☐☐		..............points
6	☐☐	< ☐☐	< ☐☐		..............points
7	☐☐	< ☐☐	< ☐☐		..............points

Total ....points

A game for two or more players, each with a copy of this score sheet.

 ▶ Roll a die six times for each set of digits, writing them in the boxes.

Game 1: If the three 2-digit numbers are in order, score 10 points; otherwise score 0 points.

Game 2: If the three 2-digit numbers are in order, score 10 points plus bonus points to match the digit in this place:

For example:

2 5 < 3 4 < 5 2   13 ....points

© 1998 Channel Four Learning Ltd **TVM Puzzle Maths**

Place Value and Ordering

1.3 Match the digits

			three hundred and seventy-two
			four hundred and sixty
			one hundred and ninety-six
			eight hundred and five
			six hundred and twenty-three
			seven hundred and forty-eight
			....
			....

A game for two or more players, each with a copy of this score sheet.

▶ Start by writing two more numbers of your own.
▶ Shuffle three sets of number cards (0 to 9) and place them face down in a pile.
▶ On your turn, turn over the top card. If you can, write the number in one of your boxes to match the words on the right.
▶ Check each other's moves.

The winner is the first to complete all their 3-digit numbers.

© 1998 Channel Four Learning Ltd **TVM Puzzle Maths**

Place Value and Ordering

1.4 Make your choice

▶ Make 3-digit numbers to fit the descriptions below, using any three of these four digits.

1. largest — | 9 | 5 | 4 |
2. smallest
3. largest odd
4. smallest even
5. largest even
6. smallest odd
7. between 530 and 550
8. between 255 and 260
9. nearest to 500
10. nearest to 600
11. nearest to 400

© 1998 Channel Four Learning Ltd **TVM Puzzle Maths**

Place Value and Ordering

Name

1.5 Words and 4-digit numbers

| 3 | 4 | 6 | 2 |

three thousand, four hundred and sixty two
7 words

| 4 | 6 | 2 | 0 |

four thousand, six hundred and twenty
6 words

▶ Write your own 4-digit numbers with these numbers of words:

7 words

6 words

5 words

4 words

2 words

Adding and Subtracting

Teacher's notes

(2.1) Making 14 page 10

Aims

To give practice in:
- adding three numbers from 1 to 10
- solving a problem by working systematically

Children can prepare for the activity by investigating pairs of numbers with a given total – for example, 10.

The activity can be approached systematically by, for example, assuming that the smallest number is 1 and deducing that the other two must total 13, so they can be 3 and 10, 4 and 9, 5 and 8, or 6 and 7. Next assume that the smallest number is 2, and so on.

Extensions
- Use the sheet to explore sets of three circles whose numbers have a different total.
- Find sets of four numbers with a given total.

(2.2) Satellite take-away game page 11

Aims

To give practice in:
- subtracting a number from 10

For children who need support, provide a tower of 10 interlocking cubes. They can then remove cubes from the tower to perform the subtraction.

A dice numbered from 1 to 10 can be used instead of cards.

Extensions
- Children can collect cubes to match the number of the planet they cover, then use them to build towers of 10, the left-over ones being left loose. When all planets have been covered, the winner is the player who has collected the most cubes.
- Create a similar game which practises subtraction from 20. Using the same cards, the planets will need to be numbered from 10 to 19.

(2.3) Animal words page 12

Aims

To give practice in:
- adding several single-digit numbers
- adding small amounts of money

The letters with their respective amounts of money can be enlarged and photocopied, then cut out to make sets of cards. The cards can then be used to spell different animals which can be displayed together with their costs.

Extensions
- Which animal is the cheapest? Which is the most expensive?
- Calculate how much change is left from 20p or 50p if different animals are bought.
- Investigate words on a different theme, such as fruits.
- Find the cost of the children, using their first names.

(2.4) Target challenge page 13

Aims

To give practice in:
- doubling numbers up to 10
- adding two or three numbers up to 16
- solving a number problem by working systematically

Prepare for the activity by practising doubling. Emphasise that double 6, for example, is 6 + 6, which can be illustrated using two towers of 6 interlocking cubes.

Children can explore different scores by placing counters in position on the target board.

Extensions
- Choose a number other than 20, and investigate different ways of making it with two or with three counters.
- What is the minimum possible score with three counters? What is the maximum? How many of the scores in between are possible?
- Suppose the outer ring counts treble. What ways of scoring 20 are there now?

(2.5) Magic squares page 14

Aims

To give practice in:
- adding three or four numbers up to 16
- finding the third of three numbers given the total and the other two

Help the children to recognise that in each magic square clues are given. In each square one line is complete, and this indicates what the magic total must be.

In a 3 × 3 magic square, the magic total is always three times the centre number.

Extensions
- Try making a magic square, without looking at the sheet, using cards 1 to 9. Start with 5 in the centre.
- Search for the relationship between the magic total and the centre number.
- Start with a magic square based on the numbers 1 to 9. Create a new 3 × 3 square by subtracting each number from 10. What do you notice?

Adding and Subtracting

2.1 Making 14

▶ In each row, find a different way to colour three circles that total 14.

(1) (2) (3) (4) (5) (6) (7) (8) (9) (10)

(1) (2) (3) (4) (5) (6) (7) (8) (9) (10)

(1) (2) (3) (4) (5) (6) (7) (8) (9) (10)

(1) (2) (3) (4) (5) (6) (7) (8) (9) (10)

(1) (2) (3) (4) (5) (6) (7) (8) (9) (10)

(1) (2) (3) (4) (5) (6) (7) (8) (9) (10)

(1) (2) (3) (4) (5) (6) (7) (8) (9) (10)

(1) (2) (3) (4) (5) (6) (7) (8) (9) (10)

(1) (2) (3) (4) (5) (6) (7) (8) (9) (10)

© 1998 Channel Four Learning Ltd **TVM Puzzle Maths**

Adding and Subtracting

2.2 Satellite take-away game

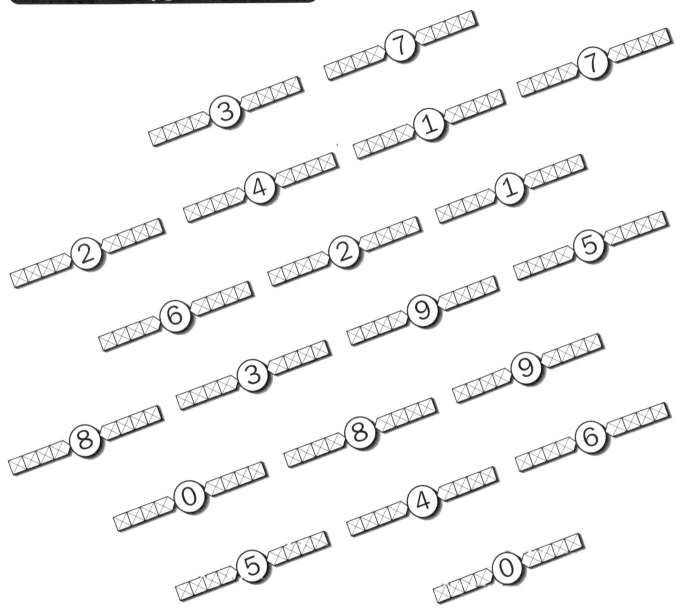

A game for two players, each with a set of counters of their own colour.

You need a pack of playing cards (without the picture cards), shuffled and placed face down in a pile.

▶ Take turns to reveal a card, take the number away from 10, and try to place a counter on a satellite that matches your answer.

The winner is the first player to cover 10 satellites.

Adding and Subtracting

2.3 Animal words

1p a	3p b	2p c	3p d	1p e	4p f	5p g
3p h	1p i	6p j	5p k	4p l	3p m	
4p n	1p o	4p p	6p q	2p r	2p s	2p t
	1p u	4p v	3p w	6p x	2p y	7p z

cat

2p	1p	2p
c	a	t

a cat costs 5p

▶ Find the costs of these animals:

dog   fox   hen

pig   goat   rabbit

Challenge

▶ Investigate the costs of other animals.

Adding and Subtracting

2.4 Target challenge

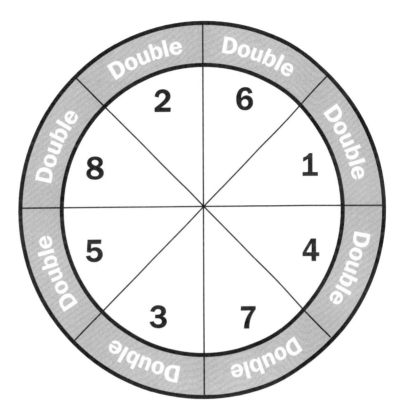

The shaded outer ring counts double.

Here are two ways of scoring 20 with two counters:

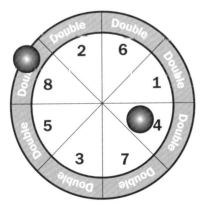   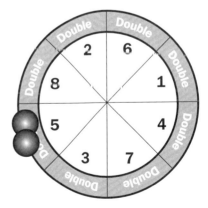

double 8, single 4   double 5, double 5

▶ How many other ways can you find of scoring 20 with two counters?
▶ Find some ways of scoring 20 with three counters.

Place counters on the target board to help you.

Adding and Subtracting

2.5 Magic squares

This is a **magic square**.

All rows, columns and main diagonals have the same total.

8	9	4
3	7	11
10	5	6

▶ Add them to check.

▶ Complete these magic squares:

6		2
	5	9
8		

3		
	6	4
		9

3	7	11
		6

	6	
	8	
5	10	

		10
		11
8		6

15	10		6
4	5	16	9
1			12

Challenge

▶ Try to make a square with cards 1 to 9 in which all eight totals are different.

Multiplying and Dividing

Teacher's notes

3.1 Fishing game page 16

Aims

To give practice in:
- dividing by 2, 5 and 10

Children can prepare for the activity by counting in 2s, 5s and 10s, starting at zero. This can be extended to recalling the ×2, ×5 and ×10 multiplication tables, in sequence and randomly.

The division facts can then be linked to the multiplication facts. For example, $3 \times 5 = 15$ – three fives are fifteen, so what is 15×5? – how many 5s make 15?

Extensions
- Investigate how many of the fish have an answer of 2, an answer of 5 and an answer of 10.
- Choose a number card, for example 6. Create different fish which have an answer of 6 ($12 \div 2$, $18 \div 3$, $30 \div 5$, and so on).
- Create an advanced fishing game involving division by other numbers.

3.2 Multiplication patterns page 17

Aims

To give practice in:
- using the concept of a multiple
- recognising patterns in the multiples of different numbers
- describing patterns

Encourage children to describe each pattern in as much detail as possible, both in terms of the arrangement of the coloured squares (columns, diagonals and so on) and in terms of the coloured numbers themselves (for example, in the ×3 grid the digits add up to 3, 6 or 9). This provides opportunites for rehearsing and consolidating mathematical vocabulary.

Although children may be most familiar with the first ten multiples, through their multiplication tables, subsequent multiples can easily be seen by continuing the pattern.

Extensions
- Try colouring the multiples of other numbers.
- Try colouring the multiples on a 1–100 square.

3.3 Doubling machine page 18

Aims

To give practice in:
- doubling 1-digit numbers
- doubling 2-digit multiples of 10
- halving numbers

The activity can be followed by making some number cards to match the numbers and their doubles. Ideally these should be differently coloured (for example, yellow for the undoubled numbers and pink for their doubles) and stuck back to back. These can be used to provide further practice in doubling, using the yellow sides and referring to the pink sides for confirmation. To practice halving, turn the cards around.

Extensions
- Extend the numbers to be doubled (and correspondingly those to be halved) to numbers between 10 and 20, and then to other 2-digit numbers.
- Construct a 'trebling machine' and create an 'in-out' table.

3.4 Grid multiplying page 19

Aims

To give practice in:
- multiplying with reference to an array of squares in a grid
- using multiplication facts up to 6×6

Make sure the children know that rows 'go across' and columns 'go down'.

Discuss the relationship between a 3×4 grid (3 rows of 4) and a 4×3 grid (4 rows of 3). Use this activity to consolidate children's understanding of the commutativity of multiplication. Children can follow up the activity by constructing their own arrays using squared paper. Pegs in a pegboard can also illustrate the concept.

Extensions
- Investigate different arrays which have the same number of squares – 12 squares, for instance.
- Construct arrays on squared paper beyond 6×6, thus extending children's range of multiplication facts.

3.5 Target 24 page 20

Aims

To give practice in:
- adding, subtracting, multiplying and dividing
- combining two or more of the operations of addition, subtraction, multiplication and division
- recalling number facts

Point out that it is acceptable to place two digits together to make a 2-digit number; and that each digit may only be used once in each expression. Note that in the example with the digits 4, 6, 2 and 1, for example, children should not be allowed to create 24 simply by joining the digits – they should include an operation.

This activity provides an opportunity to introduce children to bracket notation.

It may not be possible to make exactly 24 in each example. The children have to try and get as close as they can.

Extensions
- Try changing the target from 24 to some other number, but using the same digits.
- The activity can be made easier by giving children sets of five digits instead of four.
- Score the difference between your number and the target – for example, 0 points for making the target exactly, 2 points for making 22. The aim is to finish with a low total score.

Multiplying and Dividing

3.1 Fishing game

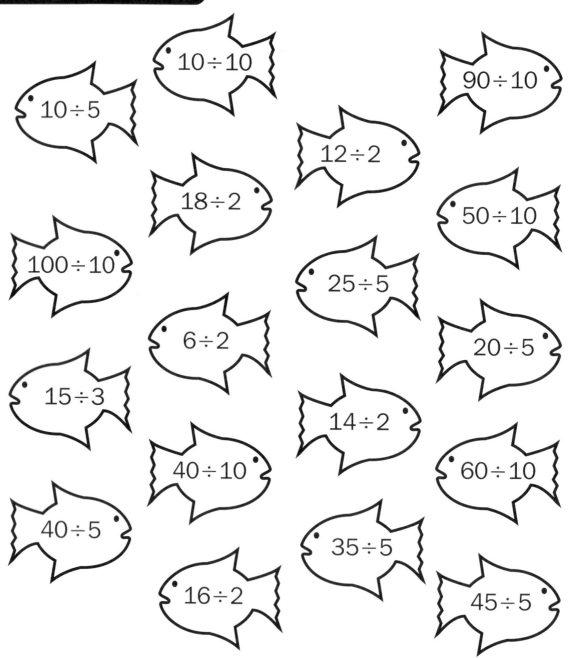

A game for two players, each with a set of counters of their own colour.

You need two sets of number cards (1 to 10), shuffled and placed face down in a pile.

▶ Take turns to reveal a card. If your card number matches the answer on a fish, catch it by placing one of your counters on top.

The winner is the first player to catch 8 fish.

Multiplying and Dividing

3.2 Multiplication patterns

▶ On each grid, colour the multiples of the number at the top.
▶ Describe any patterns you notice.

1	2	3	4	5	6
7	8	9	10	11	12
13	14	15	16	17	18
19	20	21	22	23	24
25	26	27	28	29	30
31	32	33	34	35	36

1	2	3	4	5	6
7	8	9	10	11	12
13	14	15	16	17	18
19	20	21	22	23	24
25	26	27	28	29	30
31	32	33	34	35	36

1	2	3	4	5	6
7	8	9	10	11	12
13	14	15	16	17	18
19	20	21	22	23	24
25	26	27	28	29	30
31	32	33	34	35	36

1	2	3	4	5	6
7	8	9	10	11	12
13	14	15	16	17	18
19	20	21	22	23	24
25	26	27	28	29	30
31	32	33	34	35	36

© 1998 Channel Four Learning Ltd **TVM Puzzle Maths**

Multiplying and Dividing

3.3 Doubling machine

This is a doubling machine.
When a number is fed **in**, its double comes **out**.

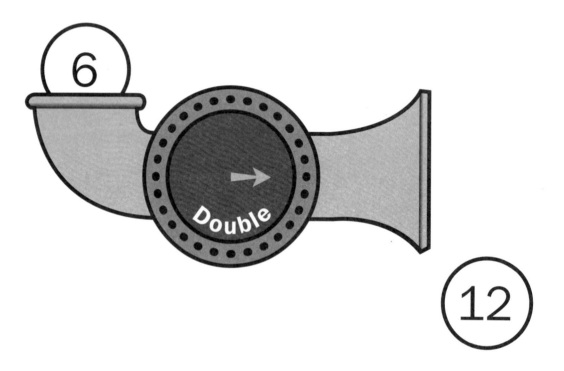

▶ Complete these tables for numbers going into and coming out of the machine.

in	6	3	9	4			2	
out	12				16	10		14

in	60	20	40			70		
out	120			160	20		60	100

Multiplying and Dividing

3.4 Grid multiplying

▶ Write a multiplication for each grid.

2 rows of 6

2 × 6 = 12

3 rows of 4

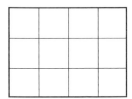

3 × 4 = 12

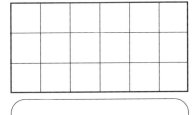

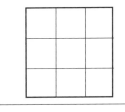

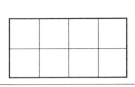

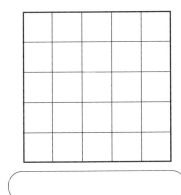

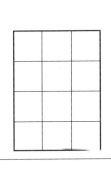

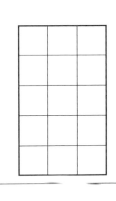

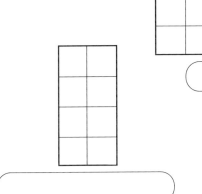

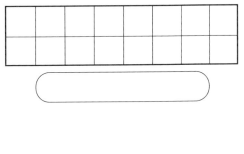

Name

Multiplying and Dividing

3.5 Target 24

▶ Use the digits given to make a number **as close as you can** to 24.
▶ How many can you make **equal to 24**?

2 7 1 5
25 − 1 = 24

4 6 2 1

8 7 6 5

3 5 2 8

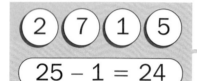

3 4 5 1

4 2 3 5

2 7 6 3

5 6 1 4

Reasoning About Numbers

Teacher's notes

4.1 Missing digits page 22

Aims
To give practice in:
- solving number problems
- making reasoned decisions based on existing knowledge
- using addition, subtraction, multiplication and division facts

The activity follows on naturally from the 'Catapult' game introduced in **Puzzle Maths** Programme 4.

Discuss with the children whether any of the problems have more than one possible solution. If not, why not?

Extensions
- Children can create their own 'missing digits' problems for others to solve.
- Children could construct 'missing digit' problems with no digits revealed; then invite another person to guess the missing digits one at a time. If they guess a correct digit, place it in its correct position; otherwise they lose a life – start with three lives.

4.2 Filling spaces page 23

Aims
To give practice in:
- solving number problems
- making reasoned decisions based on existing knowledge
- using addition, subtraction, multiplication and division facts

Discuss with the children which operations are possible in each problem. For example, in the first problem (making 12), is it possible that a space could be filled by a '+' sign? What about the other signs?

Children can be encouraged to work systematically through all the possible solutions involving addition, then subtraction, and so on.

Extensions
- How many different three-space solutions are there for 12? How many four-space and five-space solutions are there?
- Children can invent their own problems, choosing their own target number and finding all possible solutions based on three spaces, then four spaces, then five spaces.

4.3 Number machines page 24

Aims
To give practice in:
- doubling numbers up to 10
- halving even numbers up to 20
- finding a number given the result of two successive operations on it
- solving number problems

Children can be introduced to the method of trial and error – for example, try 5 as a possible number entering the first machine. Find the result (14, so 5 is too large); try another number, and so on.

A more sophisticated approach is to work backwards from the answer.

Extensions
- Create in-out tables for each machine. Try different numbers entering the machines. This could lead to discussion about negative numbers.
- The children can invent their own two-operation machines, and create in-out tables to show what happens to numbers entering them.

4.4 Questions and answers page 25

Aims
To give practice in:
- addition, subtraction, multiplication and division
- doubling and halving

Encourage children to create questions that use a variety of operations, as in the example, and also to include 'word' problems.

Extensions
- Choose different numbers as answers, then search for a range of possible questions.
- Introduce a 'daily answer'. Pick a number at random each day. The children have to say or write questions that have the day's answer.
- The questions can be restricted in order to consolidate particular ideas. For example, you could specify that the children should use the word 'multiple' in their question.

4.5 Three ways page 26

Aims
To give practice in:
- addition, subtraction, multiplication and division
- combining two or more of the operations of addition, subtraction, multiplication and division

One approach is to invite children to create as many different additions as they can, using these digits, that have an answer in the range 1 to 10; then write them on the wall. Next search for subtractions in the same way, and so on.

It may not be possible to fill all the gaps.

Extensions
- Which numbers can be made in more than three ways?
- Repeat the activity with a new set of five digits.
- Extend the numbers on the wall as far as 20.

Name

Reasoning About Numbers

4.1 Missing digits

▶ Write the missing digits in the spaces.

8 + _ = 1 7

8 − _ = 5

_ + 7 = 1 6

1 _ − 9 = 7

3 × 6 = 1 _

_ _ ÷ 3 = 4

_ × 7 = 1 _

_ × _ = 1 5

2 _ + 6 = _ 0

_ + 9 + 8 = _ 2

_ + 5 − 2 = _ 0

_ 3 + _ = 3 2

_ 1 ÷ 3 = _

5 _ − 1 1 = _ 4

22

© 1998 Channel Four Learning Ltd **TVM Puzzle Maths**

Reasoning About Numbers

4.2 Filling spaces

Each space can have a digit (0 to 9) or a sign (+, −, ×, ÷).

☐ ☐ ☐ = 1 2

Here are two ways of filling the spaces above:

2 × 6 = 1 2

9 + 3 = 1 2

▶ How many more ways can you find?

▶ Find ways to fill these spaces:

☐ ☐ ☐ ☐ − 2 2

☐ ☐ ☐ = 1 0

☐ ☐ ☐ ☐ ☐ = 4 0

Reasoning About Numbers

4.3 Number machines

▶ Write the number that enters each machine.

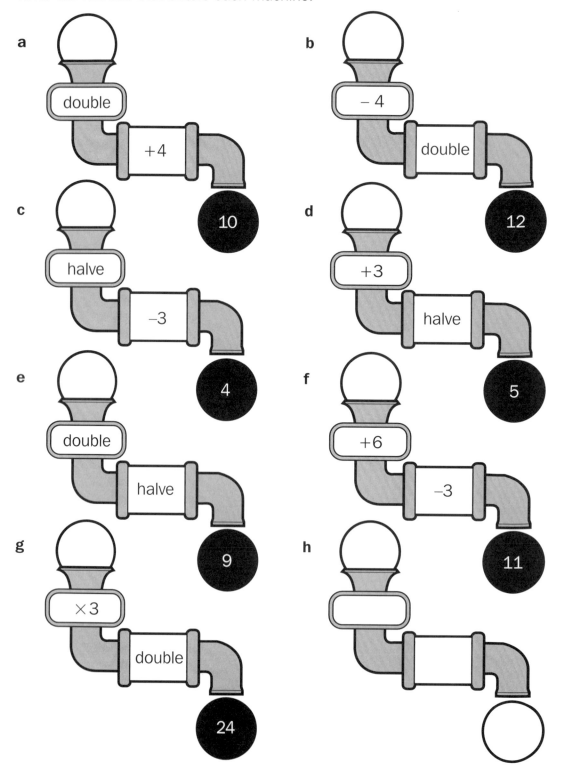

▶ Write your own numbers on the last machine.

Reasoning About Numbers

4.4 Questions and answers

Here are eight different questions with an answer of 8.

Questions

What is...?

1. 6 + 2
2. 9 − 1
3. 4 × 2
4. half of 16
5. double 4
6. the number of legs on an octopus
7. 16 ÷ 2
8. 1 + 2 + 5

▶ Write at least eight questions with each of these answers:

Answer 6   Answer 2   Answer 20

Reasoning About Numbers

4.5 Three ways

▶ Use only the digits 1, 2, 3, 4 and 7.
  Do not use any digit more than once in a box.

▶ Try to find three ways of making each of the numbers 1 to 10.
  One row is done for you.

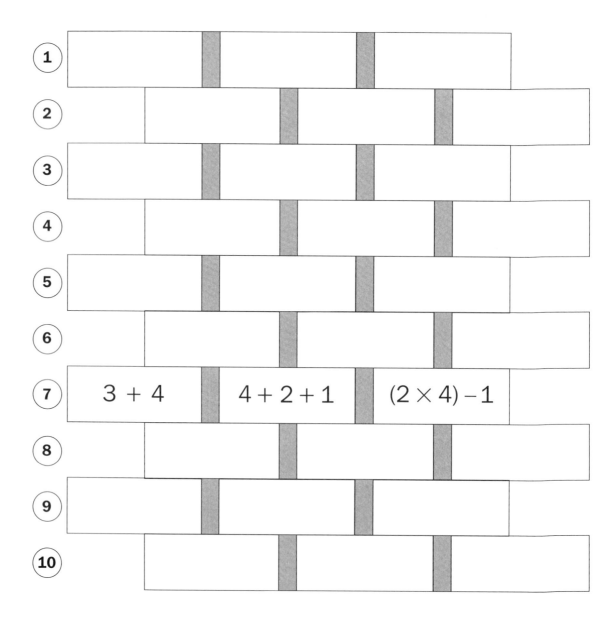

Row 7: 3 + 4 | 4 + 2 + 1 | (2 × 4) − 1

Shape and Space

Teacher's notes

5.1 Make a dice page 28

Aims

To give practice in:
- using the concept of a net of a 3-D shape
- constructing a 3-D model of a cube from a net

Ideally the net should be photocopied onto card. It could also be enlarged. Emphasise to children the need for accuracy, in the cutting and particularly in the scoring and folding. One method of scoring is to use a ruler and ball-point pen. Correct alignment of the ruler is essential to the construction of an accurate model.

Extensions
- Provide nets of other shapes for the children to construct.
- Investigate the positions of the spots on the dice – for example, consider the sum of the spots on opposite faces.
- Investigate other possible nets of a cube.

5.2 Looking for triangles page 29

Aims

To give practice in:
- recognising triangles in different orientations
- constructing triangles by shading regions
- recognising common 2-D shapes

Point out that in this activity congruent triangles in different positions are taken to be distinct.

The children can sort the triangles into types – for example, those created from one region, from two regions, and so on.

Extensions
- Investigate the creation of other shapes by colouring the regions of this grid – for example, 5-sided shapes (pentagons).
- Draw a different grid and investigate how regions may be coloured to create triangles.
- Use the colouring of regions on the grid to consolidate the concept of fractions, particularly eighths.

5.3 Tangram puzzle page 30

Aims

To give practice in:
- recognising and naming common 2-D shapes
- constructing shapes from sets of other shapes

The square is best photocopied onto card. To facilitate this process, several squares can be drawn on a single sheet of paper before photocopying.

Children should record the shapes they create, either by drawing round them or by sticking the pieces onto a backing sheet.

Extensions
- Construct other dissections of a square, and try creating other shapes using the pieces.
- Investigate the number of sides of the shapes created – is it possible to create shapes with 3 sides, 4 sides, 5 sides...? Get the children to name each shape.

5.4 Name that shape page 31

Aims

To give practice in:
- recognising and naming common 2-D shapes

Ideally you could provide children with geoboards and let them create the shapes using a rubber band.

Discuss the number of sides and the number of vertices of the shapes.

Extensions
- Provide the children with dotty paper (Resource Sheet 3, page 35). They can construct their own shapes on the geoboards and record them on the paper.
- Find the areas of some of the shapes by counting squares and half-squares.
- Investigate how many different triangles can be created on a 4 × 4 geoboard.

5.5 Perimeters page 32

Aims

To give practice in:
- finding the perimeter of shapes made up of unit squares

Discuss the meaning of perimeter. It is a length: the total distance round the boundary of a shape.

Children can try making these and other shapes using a set of card or plastic squares and joining them along their edges.

Discuss why all the perimeters are an even number of units.

Extensions
- Investigate the construction of shapes with a fixed perimeter. For example, how many shapes with a perimeter of 10 units can be made by joining unit squares?
- Calculate the areas of the shapes on the sheet.

© 1998 Channel Four Learning Ltd **TVM Puzzle Maths**

Shape and Space

5.1 Make a dice

This is a net for a dice.

▶ Photocopy it onto card, and cut it out.
▶ Score along the dotted lines, then fold and glue the tabs to make your dice.
▶ Invent a game to play with it.

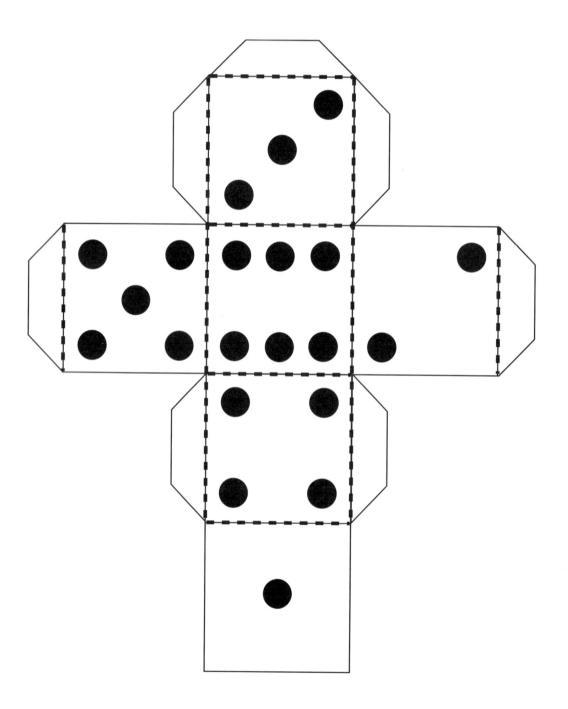

© 1998 Channel Four Learning Ltd **TVM Puzzle Maths**

Shape and Space

5.2 Looking for triangles

It is possible to colour the pattern below in 16 different ways to make a triangle. Two have been done for you.

▶ Find the others.

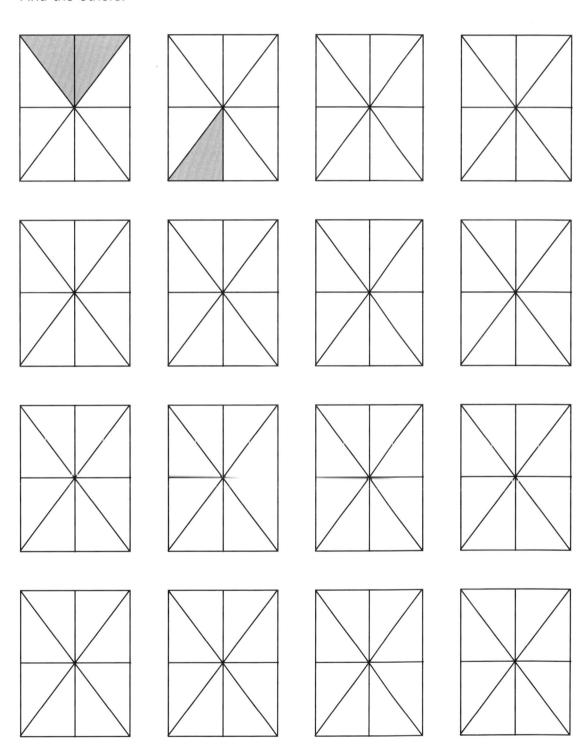

Shape and Space

5.3 Tangram puzzle

▶ Cut out a large square from card.

▶ Draw both diagonals, then cut out the four pieces.

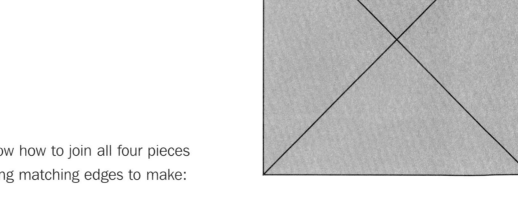

▶ Show how to join all four pieces along matching edges to make:

a square   a rectangle

a triangle   a parallelogram

a trapezium    a hexagon

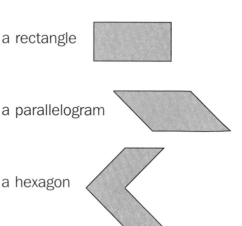

▶ What shapes can you make with just three pieces?

▶ Cut out another square like this into three pieces.

▶ See what shapes you can make with these three pieces.

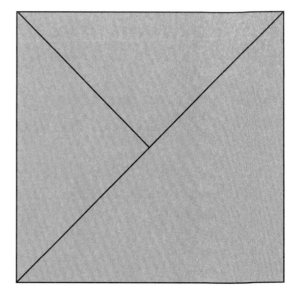

© 1998 Channel Four Learning Ltd **TVM Puzzle Maths**

Name

Shape and Space

5.4 Name that shape

▶ Write the name of each shape underneath the diagram.

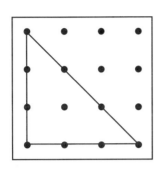
right-angled triangle

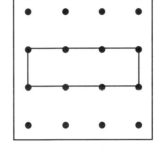
....

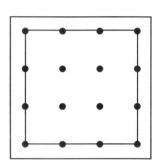
....

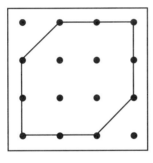
....

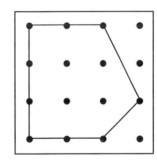
....

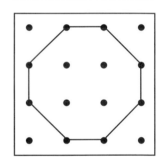
....

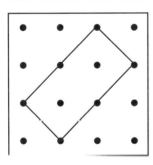
....

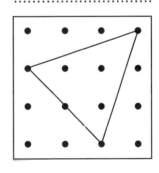
....

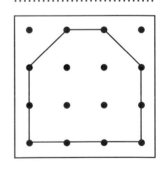
....

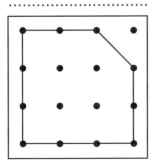
....

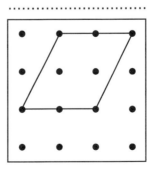
....

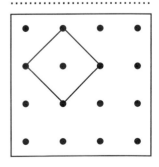
....

▶ Describe each shape and say what is special about it.

© 1998 Channel Four Learning Ltd **TVM Puzzle Maths**

Shape and Space

Name

5.5 Perimeters

▶ Write down the **perimeter** of each shape.

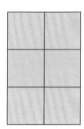

P = ... units

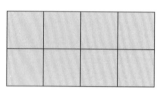

P = ... units

P = ... units

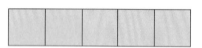

P = ... units

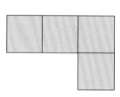

P = ... units

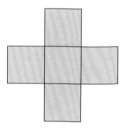

P = ... units

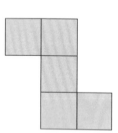

P = ... units

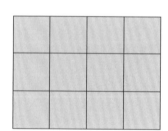

P = ... units

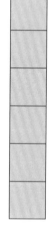

P = ... units

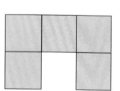

P = ... units

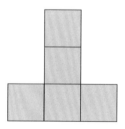

P = ... units

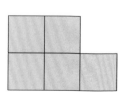

P = ... units

© 1998 Channel Four Learning Ltd **TVM Puzzle Maths**

Resource Sheet 1

1–100 square

1	2	3	4	5	6	7	8	9	10
11	12	13	14	15	16	17	18	19	20
21	22	23	24	25	26	27	28	29	30
31	32	33	34	35	36	37	38	39	40
41	42	43	44	45	46	47	48	49	50
51	52	53	54	55	56	57	58	59	60
61	62	63	64	65	66	67	68	69	70
71	72	73	74	75	76	77	78	79	80
81	82	83	84	85	86	87	88	89	90
91	92	93	94	95	96	97	98	99	100

© 1998 Channel Four Learning Ltd **TVM Puzzle Maths**

Resource Sheet 2

Number cards

0	1	2	3
4	5	6	7
8	9	10	11
12	13	14	15
16	17	18	19
20			

© 1998 Channel Four Learning Ltd **TVM Puzzle Maths**

Resource Sheet 3

Dotty grids

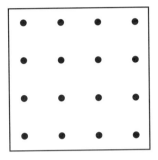 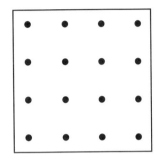 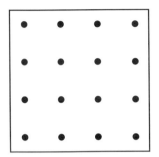

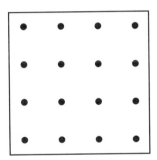 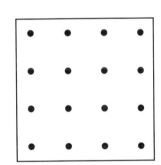 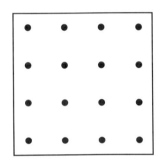

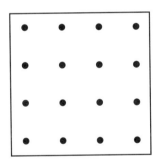 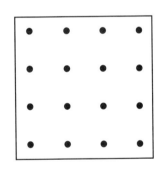 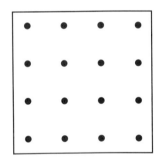

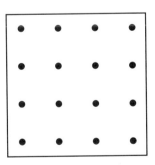 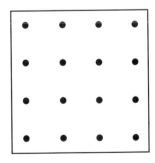 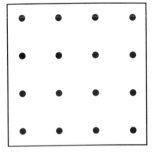

Resource Sheet 4

Multiplication patterns

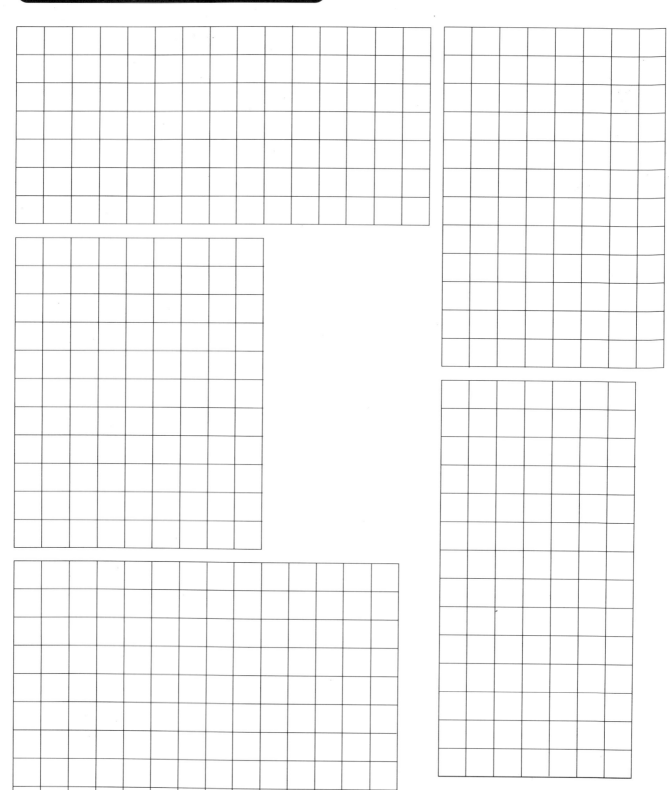